Playing the
RECORDER

GRADE 4

SHARE the Music

McGRAW-HILL

BLACKLINE MASTERS AND TEACHER'S MANUAL

SERIES AUTHORS

Judy Bond
Coordinating Author

René Boyer-Alexander

Margaret Campbelle-Holman

Marilyn Copeland Davidson
Coordinating Author

Robert de Frece

Mary Goetze
Coordinating Author

Doug Goodkin

Betsy M. Henderson

Michael Jothen

Carol King

Vincent P. Lawrence
Coordinating Author

Nancy L. T. Miller

Ivy Rawlins

Susan Snyder
Coordinating Author

Contributing Writer
Janet McMillion

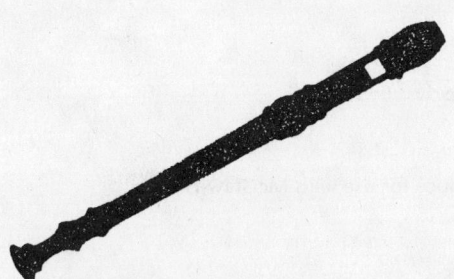

McGraw-Hill
School Division

New York   Farmington

ACKNOWLEDGMENT

Cool Mawning from DANDY SHANDY: 12 JAMAICAN FOLK-SONGS FOR CHILDREN, collected by Olive Lewin. Copyright © 1975 and reprinted by permission of Oxford University Press.

Contributing Writer
Cindy Hall

McGraw-Hill School Division
A Division of The McGraw-Hill Companies

McGraw-Hill School Division
Two Penn Plaza
New York, NY 10121

Printed in the United States of America

ISBN 0-02-295403-1 / 4

1 2 3 4 5 6 7 8 9 045 03 02 01 00 99

INTRODUCTION

Playing the Recorder, Grade 4, contains soprano recorder activities for McGraw-Hill's SHARE THE MUSIC series. The activities are in a lesson format that can be duplicated and distributed to each student participating in the classroom recorder lesson. Some teachers may wish to convert the student lesson format to overhead transparencies for use with the entire class. Teaching suggestions are provided on the back of each lesson, except in the Celebrations section.

This book teaches soprano recorder pitches D E G A B C' D' and provides activities that the student can use to practice each of the pitches. Songs are incorporated early on to provide motivation for learning, and harmony parts and ostinatos to play along with songs in the textbook are given. There are also suggestions for songs in the textbook that students can play on the recorder.

Playing the Recorder contains the following:

- Fingering charts
- Practice patterns for new pitches
- Songs, harmony parts, and ostinatos
- Opportunities for students to create their own compositions

A Celebrations section at the end of the book gives students the opportunity to extend their recorder activities with selected Celebrations songs in the SHARE THE MUSIC program.

A chart with all pitch fingerings used in *Playing the Recorder*, Grade 4, is provided on the inside back cover of this book, and staff paper that can be duplicated for various student recorder activities can be found on the last page.

All recorder activities are referenced to the appropriate place in the Teacher's Edition of SHARE THE MUSIC.

TABLE OF CONTENTS

McGraw-Hill

Name _____

"B" Is for Beginning

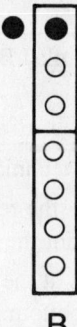

- The best way to get started playing the recorder is to jump right in! So let's begin with pitch B. Finger B with your left thumb and first finger.

B

B

- Put the mouthpiece of the recorder between your lips. Gently breathe into the recorder. Find out how long you can play B with one breath.

- To start down the road to playing the recorder, play pitch B for each line in the road map below. Play a long sound for each long line and a short sound for each short line.

Start ———— — — — — — — ———— — — — — ———— Finish

- Clap the rhythm of each pattern below. Say each rhythm with the whispered sound *dooh*. Then play the patterns on pitch B.

1. (sheet music notation)

2. (sheet music notation)

Challenge: Play a listening game with a friend: You play one of the patterns above, and your friend looks at the patterns and tries to guess which one you played. Then your friend plays a pattern, and it's your turn to guess!

Pitch: B

McGraw-Hill

USING RECORDER MASTER R•1

OBJECTIVE

- Students will learn to play B on the recorder.

PREPARATION

- Introduce these basic techniques of recorder playing:
  1. The mouthpiece of the recorder should be held between the lips, not the teeth.
  2. The left hand goes at the top of the recorder, the right hand at the bottom.
  3. The pad (flat part) of the fingers should cover the holes of the recorder. The holes should be *completely* covered.
  4. It is important to blow *lightly* into the recorder. Too much breath will result in a squeak rather than a correct pitch with good tone.

5. To produce a clean tone, whisper the word *dooh* into the recorder. This is called "tonguing." When you say *dooh,* the tongue touches the roof of the mouth just behind the front teeth. This action of the tongue starts and stops the flow of air.

- Help students make a chart of these basic recorder techniques, and post it on the classroom wall along with simple diagrams illustrating the techniques.

PROCEDURE

- Demonstrate the fingering for B on the recorder, with the left thumb covering the single hole in the back and the first (index) finger covering the top hole in the front.

- Then guide students through the activities. Be sure to check that each student is using the left hand to finger B.

EXTENSION

- Write the following patterns on the chalkboard, or write them on staff paper and duplicate for each student.

- Have students continue the practice activities by first clapping the patterns, then saying them with the syllable *dooh,* and finally playing them on pitch B.

- If time permits, add these patterns to the two on the recorder master, and have students play another version of the listening game using all four patterns.

- Have volunteers make a chart of the B fingering diagram and the B staff notation for posting on the wall. As other pitch fingerings are learned, students can make charts for the new pitches to add to the wall display for reference.

An "A" Performance

- You're ready for a new pitch! Finger B on your recorder. Then cover the next hole to finger A.

A

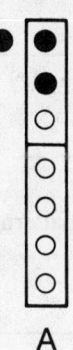

A

- Clap the rhythm below, then play the rhythm on pitch A.

- Here's a game you can play with a friend: One person names something beginning with the letter *B* or *A* that you could buy at the grocery store, then the other person plays the matching pitch, B or A. For example, if your friend names "apple," you play pitch A. Take turns choosing something to buy.

- Practice playing each of the patterns shown in the boxes.

B B B	B B A	A A A	A A B

- Now play the following rhythm patterns on A.

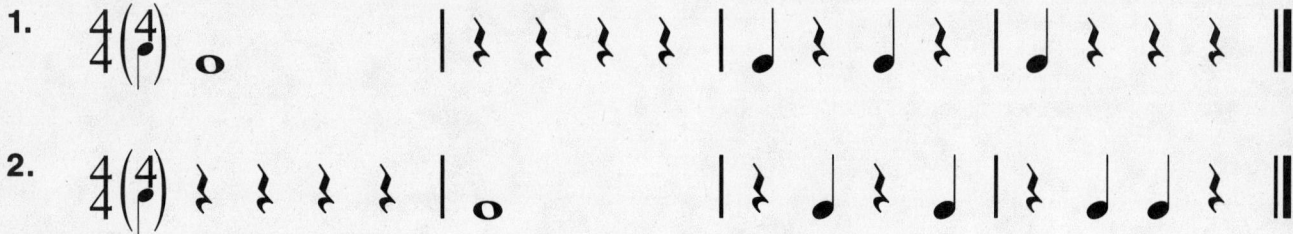

- When two performers play two parts together, it is called a **duet.** Play a duet with a friend: You play Pattern 1 above while your friend plays Pattern 2. Then switch parts and play again.

Challenge: Practice your duet until you can play it without looking at the music. Then you and your friend can play the duet for the class.

Pitches: A B

McGraw-Hill

USING RECORDER MASTER R•2

OBJECTIVE

- Students will learn to play A on the recorder and will review B.

PREPARATION

- Have students echo patterns played on B, for example:

PROCEDURE

- Demonstrate the fingering for A on the recorder by fingering B and then covering the next hole down with the second finger of the left hand.
- Guide students through the game. Help them make a list of things to buy, such as apricots, avocados, asparagus, bananas, butter, bread, beans.
- Discuss the meaning of the term *duet,* and have students practice the two patterns.

- To help students become more comfortable with playing duets, have the whole class play the duet first. Have half the class play Pattern 1 while the other half plays Pattern 2. Then have the groups switch patterns and play again.
- Help students to pair off and play the patterns as a duet.

EXTENSION

- Make copies of staff paper from the back of this book, and have students use it to write their own rhythm patterns on A, using a $\frac{4}{4}$($\frac{4}{4}$) meter signature and any of the following:

- Have students practice their patterns. Then have pairs of students combine their patterns to create a duet.

Name _____

Playing A and B

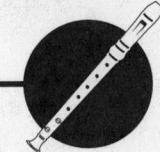

- Use the patterns below to practice playing A and B. First clap the rhythm of each pattern. Next sing or say the pitch letter names in rhythm while you finger the pitches on your recorder. Then play the patterns.

- Clap the rhythm of the song "Raindrops" below. Sing or say the pitch letter names in rhythm while fingering the recorder. Then play the song.

Raindrops

Ellen Mendelsohn

Rain - drops are fall - ing; Fall - ing on my win - dow - sill with a

pit - ter pat - ter pit - ter pat - ter. When will it stop?

- Play the song while a friend sings the words. Then switch roles and perform the song again.

Challenge: Play the rhythm of "Raindrops" on rhythm sticks, a triangle, or another percussion instrument as a friend plays the song on the recorder.

Pitches: A B

McGraw-Hill

USING RECORDER MASTER R•3

OBJECTIVE

- Students will review playing A and B on the recorder.

PREPARATION

- Have students review the fingering for A and B.

- Then have them practice moving between the two pitches.

PROCEDURE

- Guide students through the activities.

- Have a third of the class play "Raindrops" while the rest of the class sings the song. Do this several times until all students have had a chance to play.

EXTENSION

- After students have worked in pairs on the percussion accompaniment, divide the class into three groups. Have one group sing "Raindrops" while the second group plays the song on recorder and the third group plays percussion instruments.

Name _____

Become a "G" Whiz

- Once you know B and A, playing G is easy. Finger A on your recorder, then cover the next hole. You are now fingering G. Make sure the hole is completely covered.

G

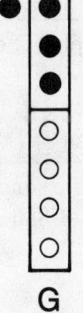

G

- Practice playing each of the patterns shown in the boxes.

| G G G | A A A | A A G | A A B |

- Clap the rhythm below, then finger each pitch.

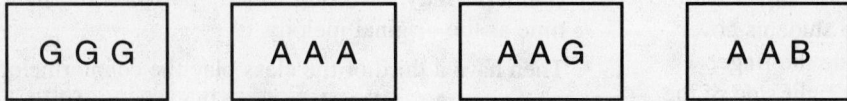

G G A A B G G A A G

- Now play the same rhythm with the melody from the staff below.

"En la feria de San Juan" Countermelody

- Play the countermelody with the refrain of "En la feria de San Juan" ("In the Market of San Juan"), on page 66 of your textbook.

Challenge: Play this mystery song. Then fill in the title.

Mystery Song: _____

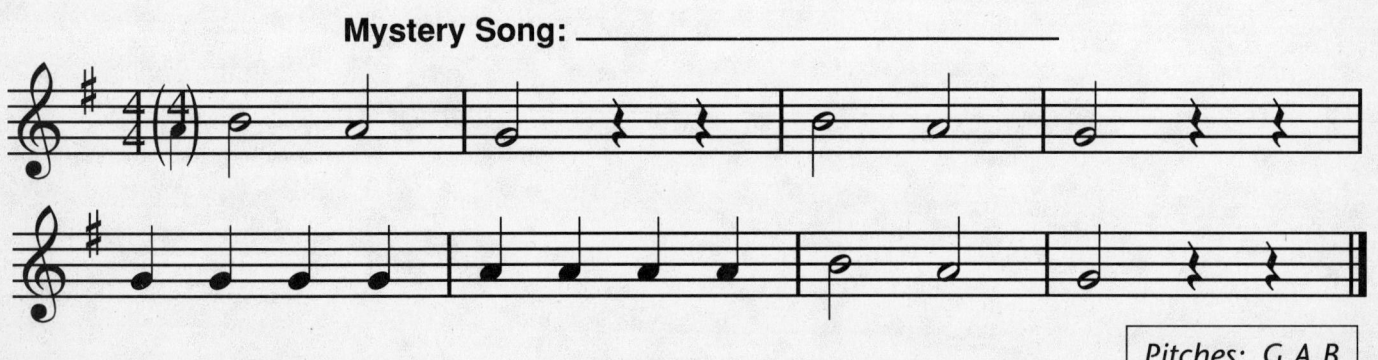

Pitches: *G A B*

McGraw-Hill

USING RECORDER MASTER R•4

OBJECTIVE

• Students will learn to play G on the recorder and will review A and B.

PREPARATION

• Have students review the song "En la feria de San Juan" ("In the Market of San Juan"), on page 66 of the textbook.

PROCEDURE

• Demonstrate the fingering for G on the recorder by fingering A and then covering the next hole down with the third finger of the left hand. To help students cover the third hole completely, have them slide the finger over until they see it sticking out on the right side of the recorder. Remind them to keep their fingers perpendicular to the recorder.

• Guide students through the activities.

• Discuss with students the meaning of the word *countermelody*: a second melody played at the same time as the original melody.

• Then have a third of the class play the countermelody while the rest of the class sings the refrain of "En la feria de San Juan."

• Have students play the mystery song and guess the title ("Hot Cross Buns").

EXTENSION

• Have students practice this accompaniment for the verse of "En la feria de San Juan":

• Then have a small group play the accompaniment with the verse and the countermelody with the refrain while the rest of the class sings the song.

McGraw-Hill

On the Trail with G A B

- Practice playing each of the patterns shown in the boxes.

| B A B | B A G | A B A | G A B |

- Write in the missing parts of the melody on the staffs below using quarter notes (♩).

"Trail to Mexico" Countermelody

B A G   G A B

G A B   B A

- Play the countermelody above with the song "Trail to Mexico," on page 59 of your textbook.

- You can write your own cowboy or cowgirl song using pitches G A B. Write the notes on the staff below, and use the rhythm given. Then exchange songs with a friend, and perform each other's song.

Challenge: Now write some words for your cowboy or cowgirl song. Sing the song while a friend plays it on the recorder.

McGraw-Hill

Pitches: G A B

USING RECORDER MASTER R•5

OBJECTIVE

• Students will review playing G A B on the recorder.

PREPARATION

• Have students echo three-note patterns using G A B, for example:

• Then have them review the song "Trail to Mexico," on page 59 of the textbook, while clapping the following ostinato, starting on the word *mind:*

PROCEDURE

• Guide students as they practice the patterns and complete the notation of the countermelody:

• Allow them time to practice the countermelody. Then listen as small groups perform the piece while the rest of the class sings "Trail to Mexico."

• Help students review the rhythm patterns written below the staff. Then guide them as they write their own songs using G A B.

EXTENSION

• Introduce students to an "arm" recorder. Have them make a fist with the right hand and place it under the chin, with the fingers toward the body. Have them place the left thumb on the inside of the right wrist and the first three fingers of the left hand on the outside of the wrist to imitate holding the recorder. Then have them practice fingering and singing patterns on G A B.

Name _____

Improvising with G A B

- Have you ever improvised your own instrument part? To **improvise** means to make something up as you go along. Here's an easy way to get started.

- Speak the words to the B section of "Down the Road," on page 76 of your textbook.

- Play the rhythm of the words on G. Then play the rhythm on A. End by playing the rhythm on B.

- Ready to improvise your own melody? Use each pitch at least once as you play different combinations of G A B to the rhythm of the words.

- Now improvise several different new melodies with the same rhythm.

- Sing the A section of "Down the Road." Improvise to the B section rhythm as you walk around the room, down an imaginary road. Then sing the A section once more.

Challenge: Write down on the staffs below one of the melodies you improvised. The rhythm is given.

Play your melody for a friend. Then play your friend's melody.

Pitches: G A B

USING RECORDER MASTER R•6

OBJECTIVE

- Students will review playing G A B on the recorder and will use the pitches in an improvisation to a given rhythm.

PREPARATION

- Have students echo four-beat patterns using G A B, for example:

$$\frac{4}{4} \, \flat \quad \natural \quad \flat \quad \natural \quad \natural \quad \| $$

  B B   A G

- Then have them review the song "Down the Road," on page 76 of the textbook.

PROCEDURE

- Guide students through the improvisation as directed. Encourage them to create a melody that they can remember.

- If time permits, have them perform their improvisations both in groups and in pairs.

EXTENSION

- See the Movement suggestions in the Teacher's Edition, page 77. Have students improvise as they walk down the alley while performing the movements for "Down the Road."

McGraw-Hill

Reviewing G A B

- Practice playing each of the following patterns.

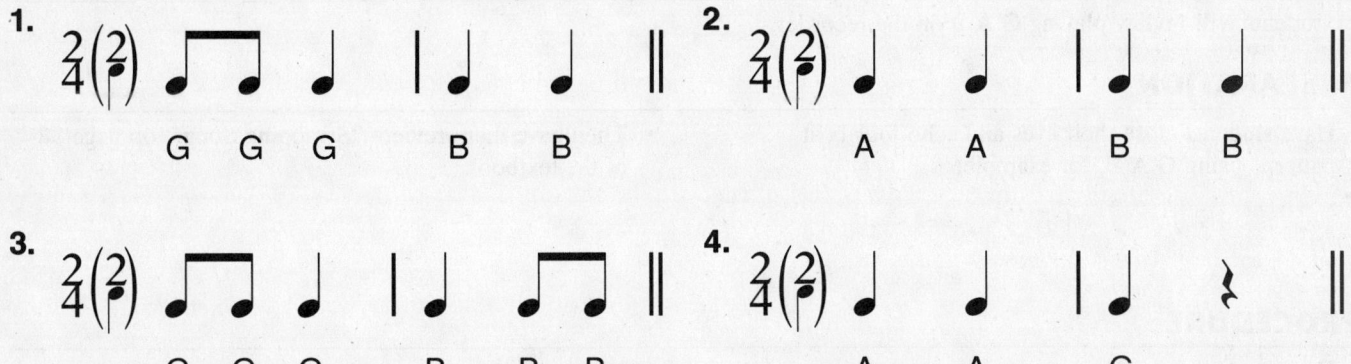

1. G G G B B
2. A A B B
3. G G G B B B
4. A A G

- Write the pitch letter name under each note on the staff below.

"Swapping Song" Accompaniment

G

- Now play the accompaniment above with the refrain of "Swapping Song," on page 82 of your textbook.

- Connect the practice patterns at the top of the page to play "Babylon's Fallin'."

Babylon's Fallin'

Virginia Folk Song

Ba - by - lon's   fall - in',   fall - in',   fall - in',

Ba - by - lon's   fall - in' to   rise   no   more.

Pitches: G A B

USING RECORDER MASTER R•7

OBJECTIVE

• Students will review playing G A B on the recorder.

PREPARATION

• Have students close their eyes and echo four-beat patterns using G A B, for example:

$$\frac{2}{4} \left(\frac{3}{4}\right) \quad \downarrow \quad \downarrow \quad | \quad \sqcap \quad \downarrow \quad \|$$
$$\qquad\quad G \quad\; G \qquad\; B\; A \quad B$$

• Then have them review "Swapping Song," on page 82 of the textbook.

PROCEDURE

• Have students practice the patterns alone.

• Then have partners use the patterns to play a "Swapping Game." One student chooses and plays one of the patterns, and the other student tries to guess which pattern it is. Then the second student chooses and plays another pattern, and the first student tries to guess which one it is. Then they trade or "swap" patterns and play each other's pattern.

• Have students completed the written activity:

| GGG | BB | AA | G |

• Then have them practice playing the accompaniment for the refrain of "Swapping Song."

• Have a third of the class play the accompaniment while the rest of the class sings the refrain of "Swapping Song." Then have students swap roles and perform again until all have played and sung.

• Have students work with partners and help each other with "Babylon's Fallin'." Then have small groups play the song while the rest of the class sings it.

EXTENSION

• Have students find and play pitches G A B whenever they occur in the refrain of "Swapping Song."

McGraw-Hill

Name _____

A "BAG" of Songs

- Play these songs using the pitches you have learned.

Merrily We Roll Along

Mer - ri - ly we roll a - long, roll a - long, roll a - long,

Mer - ri - ly we roll a - long o'er the deep blue sea.

Hot Cross Buns

Hot cross buns, Hot cross buns,

One a pen - ny, Two a pen - ny, Hot cross buns.

Ice-Cream Cone
(Variation on "Hot Cross Buns")

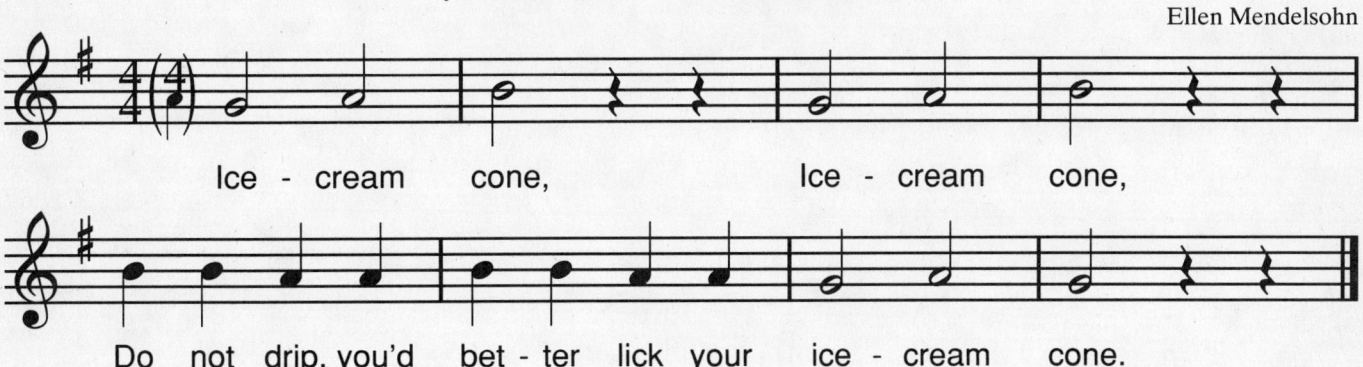

Ice - cream cone, Ice - cream cone,

Do not drip, you'd bet - ter lick your ice - cream cone.

- When you have learned the songs, play them while a friend
  sings the words.

Pitches: G A B

OBJECTIVE

- Students will play songs while reviewing G A B on the recorder.

PREPARATION

- Have students review the fingering for G A B on their recorders.

PROCEDURE

- Guide students through the following steps to help them learn each song more easily.

  1. Clap the rhythm of the song.

  2. Sing or say the letter names in rhythm while fingering the pitches on the recorder.

  3. Play the song.

EXTENSION

- Have students play each song in pairs, as a group, or as a class.

- Ask students to choose a song and practice it until they can play it without the music.

Name_____

Bird Songs in G A B

- Practice playing each of the following patterns.

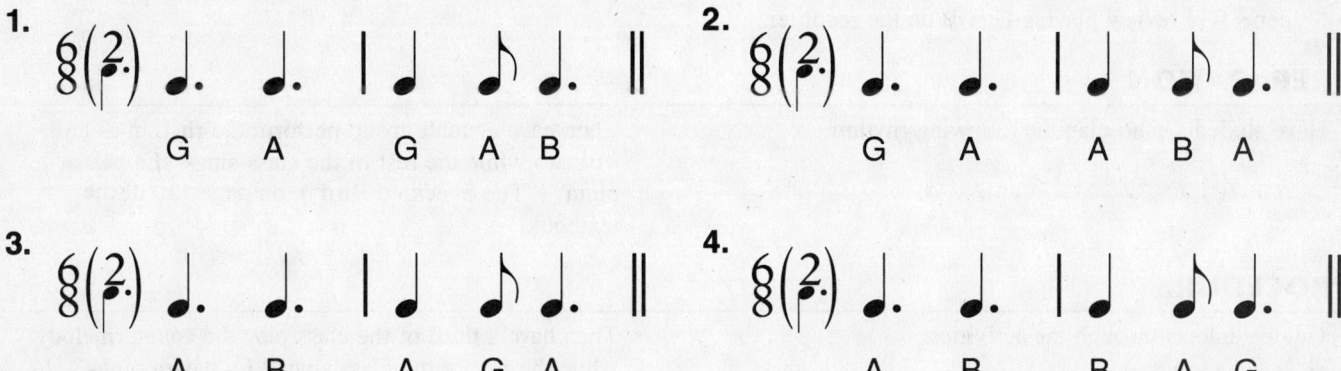

1.
G A G A B

2.
G A A B A

3.
A B A G A

4.
A B B A G

- Play the game "Mockingbird" with a friend. A mockingbird imitates
  the sounds and songs of other birds. In the game, the first person plays
  one of the patterns above. The second person is the mockingbird and
  echoes the pattern. Then you switch roles. Try all of the patterns.

- Write the pitch letter name under each note on the staffs below.

"La pájara pinta" Countermelody

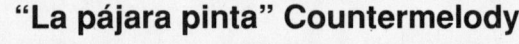

G A G A B ___ ___ ___

___ ___ ___ ___

- Now play the countermelody above with "La pájara pinta"
  ("The Speckled Bird"), on page 110 of your textbook.

Challenge: Make up your own bird song. Use the rhythm
patterns at the top of the page, but change the pitch letter names
to other combinations of G A B. Play the new patterns to see how
they sound. Then try playing your new patterns in a different
order to find the one you like best.

Pitches: G A B

McGraw-Hill

USING RECORDER MASTER R•9

OBJECTIVE
• Students will review playing G A B on the recorder.

PREPARATION
• Have students echo-clap the following rhythm:

§(²) ♩. ♩. | ♩ ♪ ♩. ‖

• Then have a small group perform the rhythm as an ostinato while the rest of the class sings "La pájara pinta" ("The Speckled Bird"), on page 110 of the textbook.

PROCEDURE
• Guide students through the activities.
• Have them fill in the pitch letter names:

| G A | G A B | G A | A B A |
A B | A G A | A B | B A G |

• Then have a third of the class play the countermelody while the rest of the class sings "La pájara pinta." Have students switch roles so all have a chance to sing and play.

EXTENSION
• Have students play the countermelody as an introduction to "La pájara pinta."

• Duplicate copies of staff paper from the back of this book, and distribute to students. Have students write on the staff paper the bird song they created. Then have them exchange papers and play their partners' bird songs.

Name_____

On the River with G A B

- Practice playing each of the following patterns.

1.

§ (♩·) ♩· ♩· | ♩· ♩· ‖

    B   A   B   G

2.

§ (♩·) ♩· ♩· | ♩· 𝄾· ‖

    A   A   B

3.

§ (♩·) ♩· ♩· | ♩· 𝄾· ‖

    A   A   G

- Now play the patterns above in this order: 1, 2, 1, 3.

- Finish writing the patterns above on the correct lines and spaces of the staffs below.

"One More River" Accompaniment

- Now play the accompaniment above with the refrain of "One More River," on page 112 of your textbook.

Pitches: G A B

USING RECORDER MASTER R•10

OBJECTIVE

• Students will review playing G A B on the recorder.

PREPARATION

• Have students sing "One More River, " on page 112 of the textbook, in the key of G. Point out to students that they will begin the song on a different pitch from the one shown on the textbook page.

PROCEDURE

• Guide students through the activities.

• Have them complete the missing part of the accompaniment:

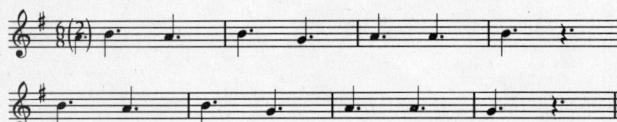

• Then listen to small groups perform the accompaniment. Choose one group to play the accompaniment while the rest of the class sings "One More River" in the key of G.

EXTENSION

• Assign students roles as the animals in the song. Have all students assigned to one animal move through the room imitating that animal while one or two students improvise an appropriate accompaniment on G A B. For example, kangaroo hops might be interpreted with staccato playing.

• Create a minidrama: verse, refrain with recorder accompaniment, verse, interlude with recorder improvisation to animal movements, verse, refrain, interlude, and so on, ending with a "rainstorm" of percussion instruments.

Name_____

A Rain"E"-Day Song

- So far you have used only your left hand to play pitches on the recorder. Now you are ready to use your right hand. Finger G on the recorder. Then place the first two fingers of your right hand on the next two holes to finger E.

E

E

- Play the "Rainstorm" below. Try playing it several different ways. How many can you find? Which do you like best?

Rainstorm

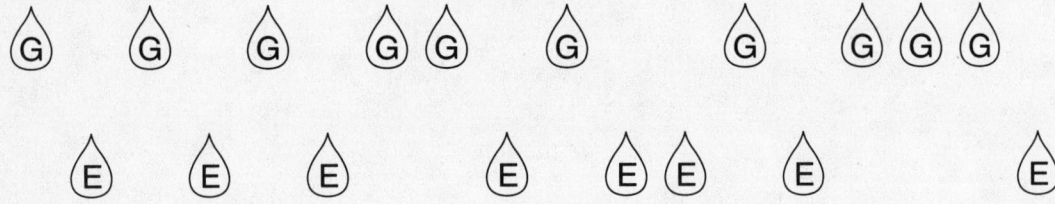

- Now practice playing each of the following patterns.

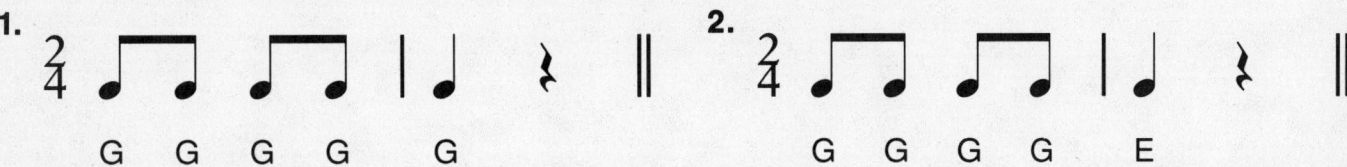

1. $\frac{2}{4}$ G G G G G

2. $\frac{2}{4}$ G G G G E

- Play the patterns above with "I Don't Care If the Rain Comes Down," on page 108 of your textbook. Instead of singing *I'm gonna dance all day,* play a pattern. Play Pattern 1 the first time, Pattern 2 the second time, Pattern 1 the third time, and Pattern 2 the fourth time.

Challenge: Use the pitches you have learned so far—E G A B— to make up a song about rain. Play your song for a friend.

Pitches: E G A B

McGraw-Hill

USING RECORDER MASTER R•11

OBJECTIVE

- Students will learn to play E on the recorder and will review G A B.

PREPARATION

- Have students review the song "I Don't Care If the Rain Comes Down," on page 108 of the textbook.

PROCEDURE

- Demonstrate the fingering for E.
- Allow students time to experiment with playing "Rainstorm," using different rhythms, dynamics, and tempos. Have them choose one version they especially like.

- Divide the class into two groups and have one group play the patterns on *I'm gonna dance all day* while the other group sings "I Don't Care If the Rain Comes Down." Then have them switch roles.

EXTENSION

- Have students use any of the pitches they have learned so far—E G A B—to write a new version of "Rainstorm." Have volunteers play their versions for the class. After

the class has listened to several versions, have students choose one or two. Write these on the chalkboard, and have students play them as a class or in small groups.

Name _____

More Rainy-Day Songs

- Play this mystery song about rain. Then fill in the title.

Mystery Song: _____

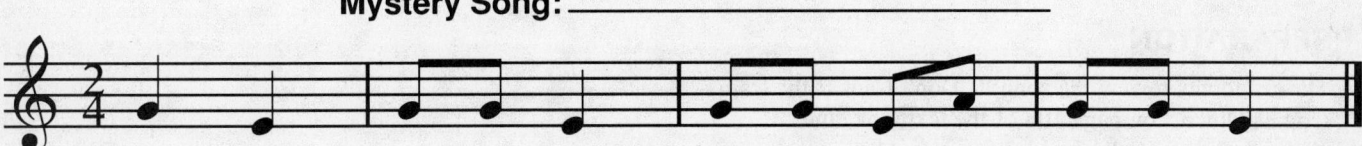

- Write the pitch letter name under each note on the staffs below.

It's Raining, It's Pouring

Traditional

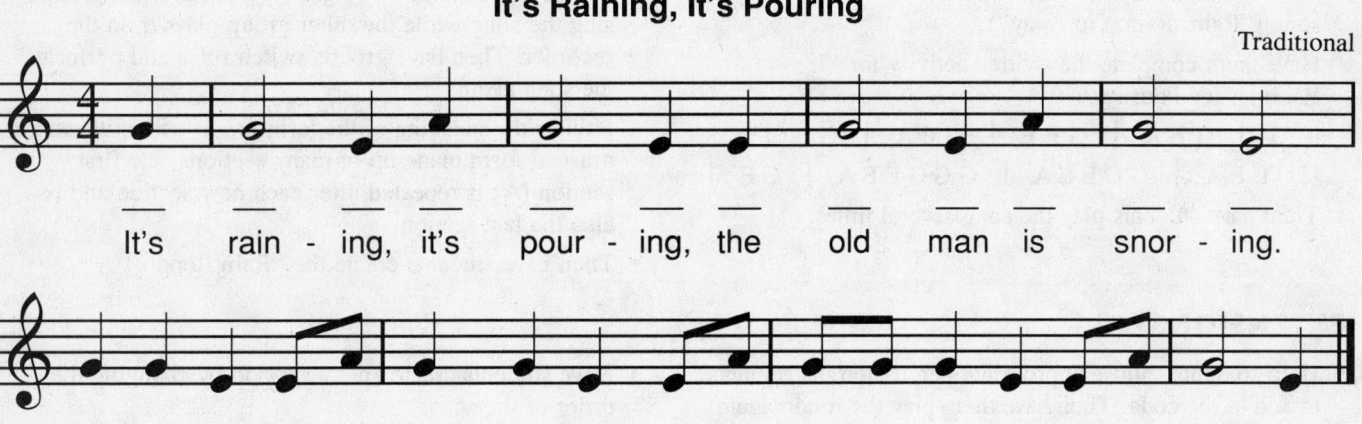

It's rain - ing, it's pour - ing, the old man is snor - ing.

Went to bed and he bumped his head, and he could-n't get up in the morn-ing.

- Now play the new rainy-day song "It's Raining, It's Pouring."

Challenge: Create a "Rain Rondo" by using "Rainstorm" and
the activity for "I Don't Care If the Rain Comes Down" on
Recorder Master R•11 together with the songs on this page.

Rain Rondo

Introduction: "Rainstorm"
       A: Sing "I Don't Care If the Rain Comes Down,"
           and play recorder on *I'm gonna dance all day.*
       B: "Mystery Song"
       A: Repeat "I Don't Care If the Rain Comes Down."
       C: "It's Raining, It's Pouring"
       A: Repeat "I Don't Care If the Rain Comes Down."
  Coda: "Rainstorm"

Pitches: E G A

USING RECORDER MASTER R•12

OBJECTIVE

• Students will review playing E G A on the recorder.

PREPARATION

• Have students review the song "I Don't Care If the Rain Comes Down," on page 108 of the textbook, and "Rainstorm" from Recorder Master R•11.

PROCEDURE

• Allow students time to play and figure out the mystery song ("Rain, Rain, Go Away").

• Have them complete the written activity for "It's Raining, It's Pouring":

  | G | GEA | GEE | GEA | GE |
GGEEA | GGEEA | GGGEEA | GE |

• Then have students play the song several times.

• Divide the class into two groups and have one group sing the song while the other group plays it on the recorder. Then have groups switch roles and perform the song again.

• Review the meaning of the term *rondo* with students: a musical form made up of many sections; the first section (A) is repeated after each new section and is also the last section.

• Then have students create the "Rain Rondo."

EXTENSION

• Help students choose appropriate percussion instruments to add to the coda. Then have them play the rondo again.

• Have students create another rondo by changing the order of the songs.

Name_____

Reviewing E G A B

- Clap the rhythm patterns below. Then play each pattern twice, first on G, then on E.

1. $\frac{4}{4}$ ♩ ♩ | ♩ ♩ ♩ :‖ **2.** $\frac{4}{4}$ ♩ ♩ ♩ | ♩ ♩ ♩ :‖

- Write the pitch letter name under each note on the staffs below.

Yangtze Boatmen's Chantey

Chinese Chantey

E   G   A   G   E   __   __   __   __   __

__   __   __   __   __   __   __   __   __   __

- Now play the melody of "Yangtze Boatmen's Chantey." A **chantey** is a song sung by sailors in rhythm with their work.

- Play a duet with a friend: One person plays Pattern 2 at the top of the page on E, four times; the other person plays "Yangtze Boatmen's Chantey."

Challenge: Practice playing each of the following patterns.

1. $\frac{6}{8}$ ($\frac{2}{8}$) ♩. ♩. | ♩. ♩. ‖   A   A   G   E

2. $\frac{6}{8}$ ($\frac{2}{8}$) ♩. ♩. | ♩. 𝄽. ‖   A   A   G

3. $\frac{6}{8}$ ($\frac{2}{8}$) ♩. ♩. | ♩. ♩. ‖   A   A   G   E

4. $\frac{6}{8}$ ($\frac{2}{8}$) ♩. ♩. | ♩. 𝄽. ‖   E   G   A

On page 132 of your textbook there is another chantey, "I's the B'y." Play the patterns above in order with the verse of the song.

Pitches: E G A B

McGraw-Hill

USING RECORDER MASTER R•13

OBJECTIVE

- Students will review playing E G A B on the recorder.

PREPARATION

- Have students sing the song "I's the By," on page 132 of the textbook.

PROCEDURE

- Allow students time to practice the patterns at the top of the page.
- Have them complete the written activity:

  | EG | AGE | EG | AGE |
  | BAG | BAG | EG | AGE |

- Then have them play "Yangtze Boatmen's Chantey."

- Review the definition of the term *duet* introduced on Recorder Master R•2.
- Then listen as partners play their "Yangtze Boatmen's Chantey" duets.
- Have all students practice the "I's the B'y" patterns. Then have a small group play the patterns while the rest of the class sings the verse of the song.

EXTENSION

- Have students play the "I's the B'y" patterns as an introduction to the song.

McGraw-Hill

Down South with E G A

- Practice playing each of the patterns shown in the boxes.

| G A G | | G E G | | G G A A G | | G E E G |

- Write each note on the staff below to the rhythm given. Then play the melody of "Arre, mi burrito."

Arre, mi burrito

New Mexico Folk Song

G G A A G E E G G A A G

- Clap the new rhythm below.

- Now play the melody of "Arre, mi burrito" with the new rhythm:

Challenge: Pat the rhythm of the A section of "La raspa" (also known as "Mexican Hat Dance") below. Then make up your own melody for the rhythm using pitches E G A.

Pitches: E G A

McGraw-Hill

OBJECTIVE

• Students will review playing E G A on the recorder.

PREPARATION

• Have students close their eyes and echo patterns on
  E G A. The patterns should be given in $\frac{2}{4}$ and $\binom{6}{8}\binom{2}{\cdot}$
  meters, for example:

PROCEDURE

• Guide students through the activities.

• Have them complete the melody of "Arre, mi burrito"
  on the staff:

• Have students add a bongo drum ostinato to the $\binom{6}{8}\binom{2}{\cdot}$
  version of the melody:

EXTENSION

• Have students share their "La raspa" melodies. Notate
  one student's melody on the chalkboard, and have all
  students play it.

Patterns with E G A

- Clap the rhythm below. Then play it on pitch E.

- Now practice playing each of the following patterns.

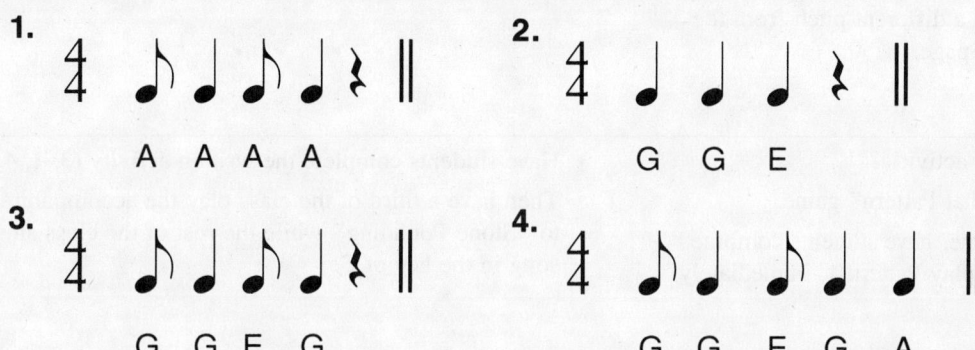

1.
A A A A

2.
G G E

3.
G G E G

4.
G G E G A

- Play "Name That Pattern" with a friend: One person plays one of the patterns above, and the other person tells the number of the pattern. Then switch roles and play the game again.

- The patterns above are shown in a different order on the staffs below. Write the number of the pattern in the box below each measure.

"Stone Pounding" Accompaniment

Play three times

- Now play the accompaniment above with the song "Stone Pounding," on page 160 of your textbook.

Pitches: *E G A*

USING RECORDER MASTER R•15

OBJECTIVE

- Students will review playing E G A on the recorder.

PREPARATION

- Have students sing "Stone Pounding," on page 160 of the textbook, in the key of C. Point out to students that they will begin the song on a different pitch from the one shown on the textbook page.

- Then have them echo four-beat patterns played on E G A, for example:

PROCEDURE

- Guide students through the activities.

- Demonstrate the "Name That Pattern" game.

- For a more challenging game, have students combine two patterns; for example, play Pattern 1, immediately followed by Pattern 3.

- Have students complete the written activity (3, 1, 4, 2).

- Then have a third of the class play the accompaniment to "Stone Pounding" while the rest of the class sings the song in the key of C.

EXTENSION

- Have students play "Pass the Pattern." For this, groups of four or five players sit in small circles. The leader plays one of the four patterns. Then the student sitting to the left of the leader plays the same pattern. The next student to the left does the same, and this is repeated until all have played the pattern. Then a member of the group identifies the number of the pattern and chooses another pattern to play. The game continues until all the patterns have been played.

Name _____

Building a House with E G A

- Clap each of the following rhythm patterns.

- Using pitches E G A, create your own melody on the staffs below for each of the rhythms.

- Play your patterns in order.

- Now you and a friend play your patterns one after the other to make a new composition.

- Write the letter name of each pitch under the notes on the staffs below.

"Hosanna, Me Build a House" Countermelody

     G   G   G   A   — — —   —

— — —   — — — —   —

- Now play the countermelody above with the A section of "Hosanna, Me Build a House," on page 164 of your textbook.

Pitches: E G A

USING RECORDER MASTER R•16

OBJECTIVE

• Students will review playing E G A on the recorder.

PREPARATION

• Have students walk through the room to the steady quarter-note rhythm of a drum. Then have them change the speed of their steps as you play half notes, eighth notes, and whole notes.

PROCEDURE

• Guide students through the activities.

• Let students share the patterns they created. Have the class choose one or two, and write these on the chalkboard for the class to play.

• Have students complete the written activity:

| GGG | A | GGG | A |
GGG | A | GGGGG | E |

• Then have a small group of students play the countermelody while the rest of the class sings the A section of "Hosanna, Me Build a House," on page 164 of the textbook.

EXTENSION

• Assign the name of a tool to each of the patterns at the top of the page:

1. hammer   2. screwdriver

3. saw   4. paintbrush

Have some students pantomime using each of the tools while others play the corresponding pattern. Have students use this activity as an interlude between repetitions of "Hosanna, Me Build a House."

McGraw-Hill

Name _____

Playing a Jamaican Melody

- Clap the rhythm of each of the patterns below.

- Now clap the following rhythm. Then play it on pitch B.

- Improvise a melody to the rhythm above using pitches G A B.

- Now improvise another melody, adding pitch E.

- Write the pitch letter name under each note on the staffs below. Then practice playing the melody of this Jamaican folk song.

Cool Mawning

Jamaican Folk Song

B B A G A __ __ __ __

__ __ __ __ __ __ __

Challenge: When this folk song is played at Jamaican festivals, people sing, dance, and play drums. Work with some of your classmates to improvise drum rhythms to go with the melody. Some of you play the melody on the recorder while the others improvise rhythms. Then create some dance steps to perform to the melody.

Pitches: E G A B

McGraw-Hill

USING RECORDER MASTER R•17

OBJECTIVE

• Students will review playing E G A B on the recorder.

PREPARATION

• Have students echo four-beat patterns using E G A B, for example:

PROCEDURE

• Guide students through the activities, assisting with the reading of the rhythm patterns.

• Have them complete the written activity:

| B B A G A | G E E G | A | B G G G |
| G G E G A | G E E G | A | B G G G |

• Help students form groups to improvise drum rhythms and dance steps.

EXTENSION

• Have students add this accompaniment to "Cool Mawning":

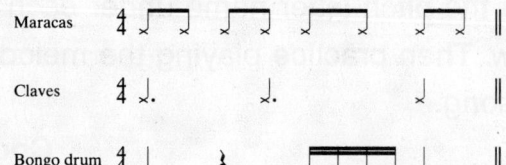

Canoe with You and E A B

- Clap the following rhythm.

- Play the rhythm above three times:

    1. on A   **2.** on E   **3.** switching between E and A

- Now practice playing each of the patterns shown in the boxes.

E E A B A	A A A B A	B B A B	A A E A

- Write the pitch letter name under each note on the staffs below.

"Hoe Ana Te Vaka" Accompaniment

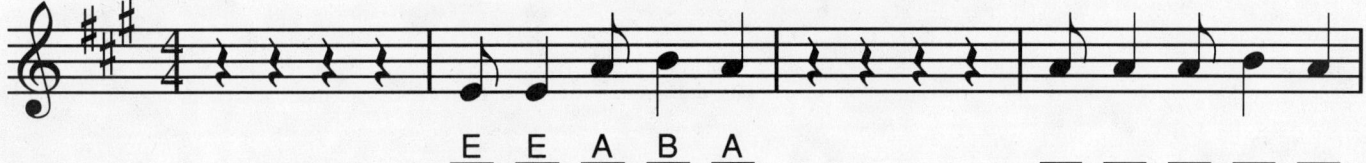

E E A B A   _ _ _ _ _

_ _ _ _ _   _ _ _ _   _ _ _ _

- Now practice playing the accompaniment above with the two
  A sections of "Hoe Ana Te Vaka" ("Paddle the Canoe"), on
  page 181 of your textbook.

Challenge: Work with a friend to create an introduction for "Hoe
Ana Te Vaka." Use the rhythm at the top of the page and pitches
E A B. Try playing the pitches in different orders. Choose the one
you like best, write it down, and practice playing it with your friend.

Pitches: E A B

USING RECORDER MASTER R•18

OBJECTIVE

• Students will review playing E A B on the recorder.

PREPARATION

• Have students echo rhythm patterns using E A B, for example:

$$\begin{array}{c} \frac{4}{4} \quad \eighthnote \quad \quarternote \quad \quad \eighthnote \quad \quarternote \quad \quad \quarternote \quad \| \\ \text{A} \quad \text{B} \quad \text{A} \quad \text{E} \quad \text{E} \end{array}$$

PROCEDURE

• Guide students through the activities.

• Have them fill in the pitch letter names for the accompaniment:

| E E A B A | A A A B A |
B B A | B B B A | B | A A E A |

• Then have a third of the class play the accompaniment while the rest of the class sings "Hoe Ana Te Vaka" ("Paddle the Canoe"), on page 181 of the textbook.

EXTENSION

• Have partners play the introductions they created. Have the class choose one of the introductions, and write the pattern on the chalkboard. Then have a third of the class play the introduction and the accompaniment while the rest of the class sings "Hoe Ana Te Vaka."

McGraw-Hill

A Starry Night with E G A B

- Clap the rhythm of each of the following patterns. Then play the patterns on pitch E.

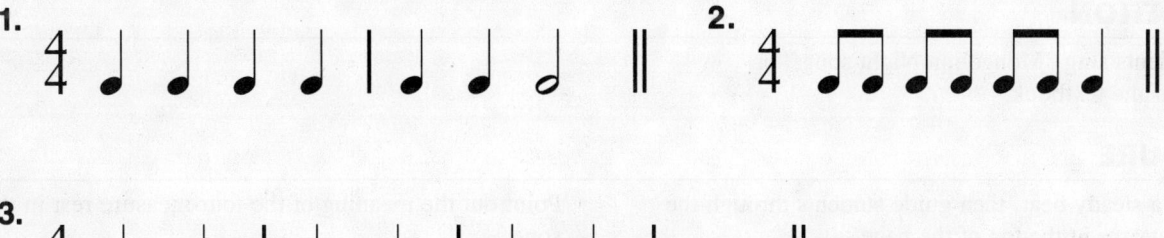

- Speak the letter name of each pitch in Part 1 below in rhythm. Then play the part. Do the same for Part 2 and Part 3.

"Mongolian Night Song" Introduction

- Form your own recorder ensemble, or group. Choose two friends and play all three parts above together.

- Now play the three parts together again as an introduction to "Mongolian Night Song," on page 19 of your textbook. After playing the introduction, sing the song.

Challenge: Clap the rhythm of "Mongolian Night Song." Then practice playing the melody of the song.

Pitches: E G A B

USING RECORDER MASTER R•19

OBJECTIVE

- Students will review playing E G A B on the recorder.

PREPARATION

- Have students sing "Mongolian Night song," on page 19 of the textbook.

PROCEDURE

- Establish a steady beat, then guide students through the rhythm patterns at the top of the page.

- Assist in dividing students into groups of three to perform the introduction.

- Point out the meaning of the four-measure rest in the song.

- For a final performance, have a third of the students play the song while the rest of the class sings it.

EXTENSION

- Have students say, in rhythm, the words *In the moonlight's golden glow, Soft the wind begins to blow.*

- Have each student compose a melody to the rhythm of the words, using E G A B. Melodies can be shared individually or performed as an interlude between verses of the song.

Name _____

Little David from Harp to Recorder

- Play these pitches floating from Little David's harp.

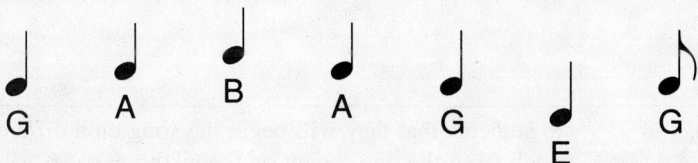

G   A   B   A   G   E   G

- Write the notes for the same pitches on the staff below. Use quarter notes.

"Little David, Play on Your Harp" Accompaniment

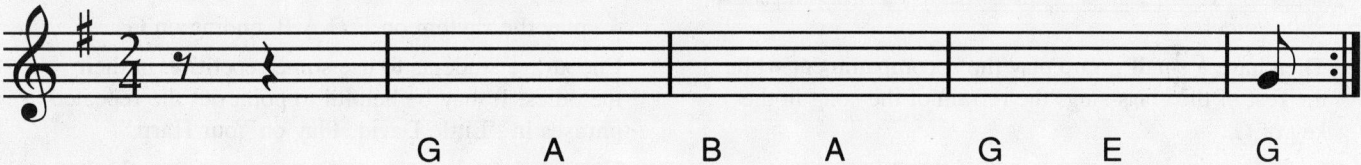

G   A   B   A   G   E   G

- Play the accompaniment above with the refrain of "Little David, Play on Your Harp," on page 168 of your textbook.

- Now compose a new piece using pitches E G A B and the rhythm below.

Challenge: With three friends, combine all the pieces you composed into a song. Work together to write words for the song and to decide how to perform the piece. Decide who will play and who will sing. Will you use an introduction, interlude, or accompaniment?

Pitches: E G A B

USING RECORDER MASTER R•20

OBJECTIVE

- Students will review playing E G A B on the recorder and will use the pitches to compose an original piece.

PREPARATION

- Have students sing "Little David, Play on Your Harp," on page 168 of the textbook, in the key of G. Point out to students that they will begin the song on a different pitch from the one shown on the textbook page.

PROCEDURE

- Guide students through the activities.
- Have them write the pitches of the accompaniment on the staff:

- Then have a small group play the accompaniment while the rest of the class sings the refrain of the song in the key of G.

- To help students with their compositions, have them:
  1. clap the rhythm together
  2. play the rhythm on G
  3. play the rhythm on G A B, ending on G
  4. play the rhythm on E G A B, ending on G

  Encourage students to use some repetition in their melodies. It may be helpful to point out the repeated phrases in "Little David, Play on Your Harp."
- Have students listen to and compare one another's melodies.

EXTENSION

- Choose one of the compositions, and have students play it as an introduction to "Little David, Play on Your Harp."

Name _____

Learning to Play D "D"lightfully

- Try a new pitch! Finger E on your recorder. Then cover the next hole to finger D.

D

D

- Clap the rhythm below. Then practice playing the rhythm on D.

$\frac{3}{4}$ 𝅗𝅥. | 𝅗𝅥. | 𝅗𝅥 ♩ | 𝅗𝅥. ‖

- Practice playing each of the patterns shown in the boxes.

| D D E | | E E D | | E D E | | D E D |

- Write the pitch letter name under each note on the staffs below. Then practice playing the part.

"Tum-Balalaika" Accompaniment

- Now play the accompaniment above with the refrain of "Tum-Balalaika," on page 210 of your textbook.

Pitches: D E

41

USING RECORDER MASTER R•21

OBJECTIVE

- Students will learn to play low D on the recorder and will review E.

PREPARATION

- Have students echo patterns on E, for example:

PROCEDURE

- Demonstrate the fingering for low D by fingering E and then covering the next hole down with the third finger of the right hand. Have students push their finger across the recorder until the hole is completely covered.
- Guide students through the activities.

- Have them fill in the pitch letter names of the accompaniment:

| D | D | DD | E | E | E | EE | D |
| D | D | DD | D | E | E | EE | D |

- Then have a third of the class play the accompaniment while the rest of the class sings the refrain of "Tum-Balalaika," on page 210 of the textbook.

EXTENSION

- Have students use pitches D and E to create a four-measure introduction and interlude for "Tum-Balalaika."

Then have them take turns playing their compositions on repetitions of the song.

Name_____

Learning a Lullaby

- Play "Head and Shoulders" with a friend: When you touch your head, your friend plays E; when you touch your shoulders, your friend plays D. Then switch roles.

- Play the pattern below on E, then on D.

- Write *E* or *D* in any order in each blank below. Then play the pattern.

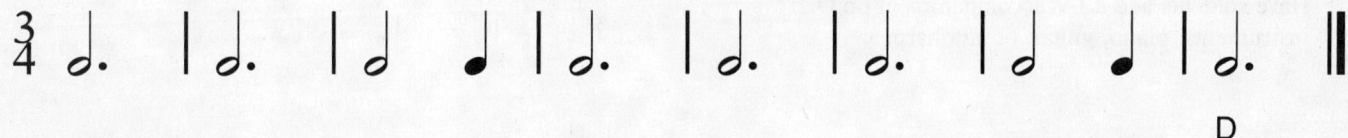

____ ____ ____ ____ ____ ____ ____ ____ ____ ____ ____ D

- Now try playing the lullaby "Fais do-do" below.

Fais do-do

French Folk Song

- Play a duet with a friend: Your friend plays "Fais do-do" above, and you play the pattern you wrote above on E and D. Then switch parts and play again.

Challenge: Practice "Fais do-do" until you can play it without the music.

McGraw-Hill

Pitches: D E G A B

USING RECORDER MASTER R•22

OBJECTIVE

- Students will review playing D E G A B on the recorder.

PREPARATION

- Have students review the fingering for low D.

PROCEDURE

- Help students find partners for "Head and Shoulders," then demonstrate the game. The students performing the movements should do them as fast as the recorder players can respond.

- Guide students through the rest of the activities.
- Have the class listen to the duets.

EXTENSION

- Have students add a I-V accompaniment on Orff instruments, piano, guitar, or autoharp:

Clap, Pat, and Stamp for D E G

- Play a body-percussion game, "Clap, Pat, Stamp," with a friend.

  Clap means G.   *Pat* means E.   *Stamp* means D.

  One person begins by performing three body-percussion sounds.
  The other person plays the matching three pitches. For
  example, if your friend performs pat, pat, clap, you play E E G.

- Practice playing each of the patterns below, then write the
  patterns on the staffs.

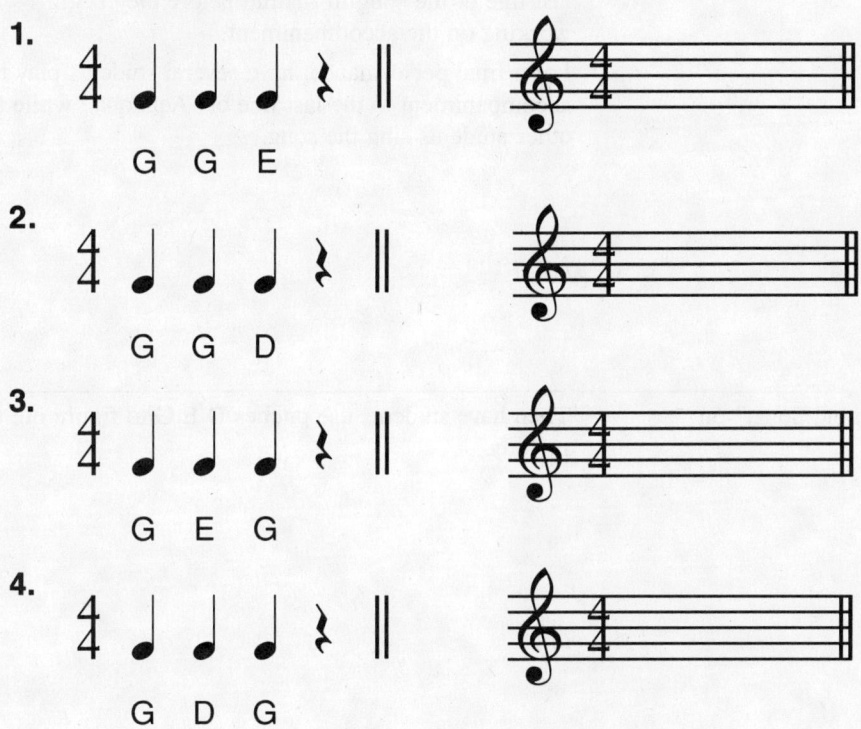

1. G G E

2. G G D

3. G E G

4. G D G

- Say the letter name of each pitch in the pattern below as you
  finger the pitches on your recorder. Then play the pattern.

"Aquaqua" Accompaniment

G E   G E   G   E G E G D G   E

- Now play the pattern as an accompaniment to the last line of
  "Aquaqua," on page 219 of your textbook.

Pitches: D E G

USING RECORDER MASTER R•23

OBJECTIVE

- Students will review playing D E G on the recorder.

PREPARATION

- Have students echo four-beat patterns using D E G, for example:

PROCEDURE

- Introduce the game "Clap, Pat, Stamp."
- Guide students through the practice and notation of the patterns:

1.

2.

3.

4.

- Have students review the song "Aquaqua," on page 219 of the textbook. Then have them say the words of the last line of the song in rhythm before they begin working on the accompaniment.

- For a final performance, have several students play the accompaniment to the last line of "Aquaqua" while the other students sing the song.

EXTENSION

- Have students sing the verse of "Swapping Song," on page 82 of the textbook.

- Then have students use pitches D E G to figure out the melody.

Signs of the Road with D E G A B

- Follow the road signs below, and play each pattern.

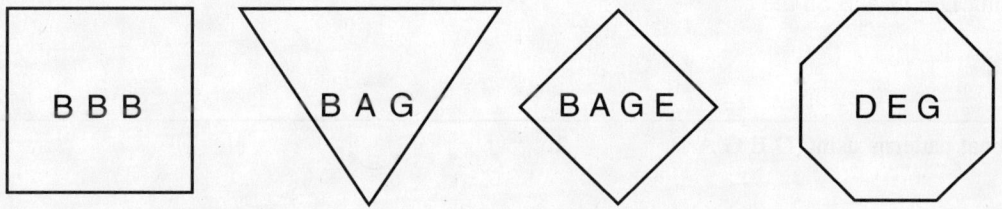

- Sing the song "Down the Road," on page 76 of your textbook.

- Now practice playing the following pattern, beginning slowly and building up to the song tempo.

Come a-long and walk to-geth - er

- Play the A section of "Down the Road." Then improvise to the rhythm of the B section using pitches D E G A B.

- Now play the accompaniment below together with the A section of the song.

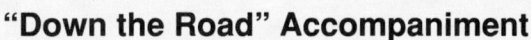
"Down the Road" Accompaniment

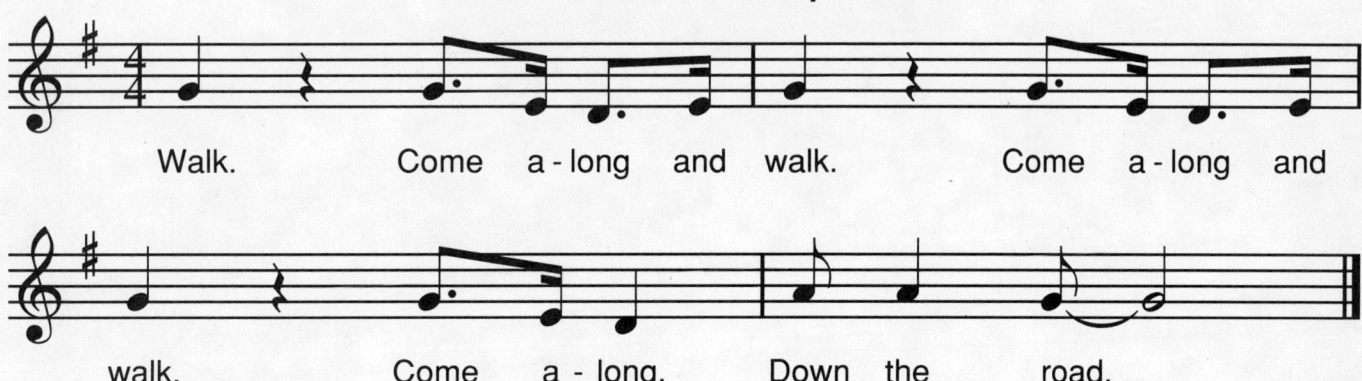

Walk.   Come a - long and walk.   Come a - long and

walk.   Come a - long.   Down the   road. ___

Challenge: Play the song "Oh, Won't You Sit Down?" on page 2 of your textbook.

Pitches: *D E G A B*

USING RECORDER MASTER R•24

OBJECTIVE

- Students will review playing D E G A B on the recorder.

PREPARATION

- Have students echo four-beat patterns using D E G A B, for example:

1. 4/4 ♩ ♩ ♩ ♩ ‖
   B B A G

2. 4/4 ♪ ♩ ♪ ♩ 𝄽 ‖
   D E   G

PROCEDURE

- Guide students through the activities.
- To help students with the improvisation, have them:

1. Speak the words to the B section of "Down the Road," on page 76 of the textbook.

2. Play the rhythm of the words on each of pitches D E G A B.

3. Use each pitch at least once as they play different combinations of D E G A B to the rhythm of the words.

4. Improvise several different new melodies.

EXTENSION

- Have volunteers play their improvisations for the class.
- Have students help you notate one of the improvisations on the chalkboard.

- Then have a small group play the A section accompaniment at the bottom of the page followed by the B section composition on the chalkboard while the rest of the class sings the A section of the song and claps the rhythm of the B section.

McGraw-Hill

Name _____

A Duet with D E G A B

- Practice playing each of the patterns shown in the boxes.

| G E G | A E A | G D G | A D A |

- Clap the rhythm of the pattern below, then play the pattern.

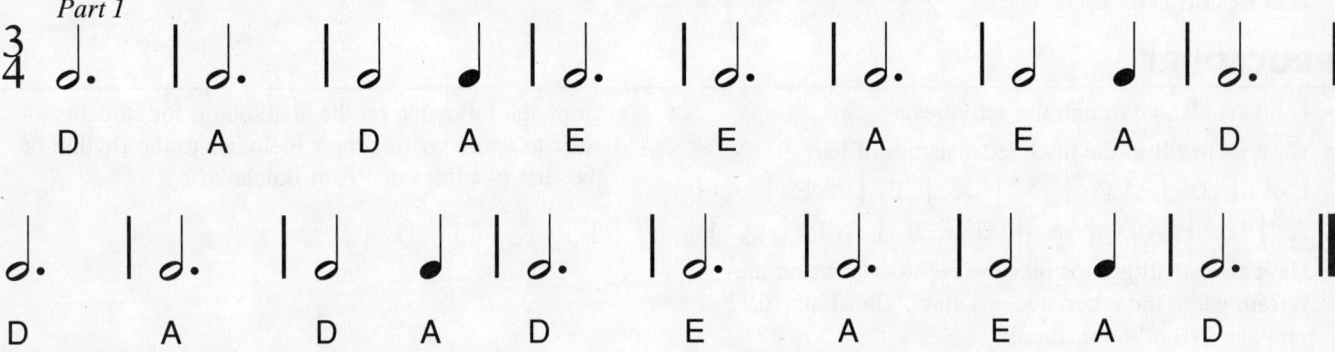

Part 1

3/4

D A D A E E A E A D

D A D A D E A E A D

- Write the letter name of each pitch under the notes on the
  staffs below. Then play the pattern.

Part 2

- With a friend, play both of the above parts together as a duet.

- Now play the parts with the refrain of "Tum-Balalaika," on
  page 210 of your textbook.

Challenge: Write your own melody, using pitches D E G A B, to
the rhythm of the first two lines of "Tum-Balalaika." Begin and
end the melody with pitch E, and end the first line with pitch B.

Pitches: D E G A B

McGraw-Hill

OBJECTIVE

- Students will review playing D E G A B on the
  recorder.

PREPARATION

- Have students echo the following patterns: G E G,
  E D E, G E D, D E G.

PROCEDURE

- Guide students through the activities.
- Have them fill in the pitch letter names of Part 2:

  | A | D | AD | A | A | E | AE | A |

  A | D | AD | A | G | E | AE | A |

- Have two small groups play the recorder parts on the
  refrain while the other students sing "Tum-Balalaika,"
  on page 210 of the textbook.

- Copy the following on the chalkboard for students to
  refer to while writing their melodies to the rhythm of
  the first two lines of "Tum-Balalaika":

EXTENSION

- Have students perform their melodies as an introduction
  to the song and as an interlude between repetitions.

Name_____

Write Your Own Melody with D E G A B

- Practice playing each of the following patterns.

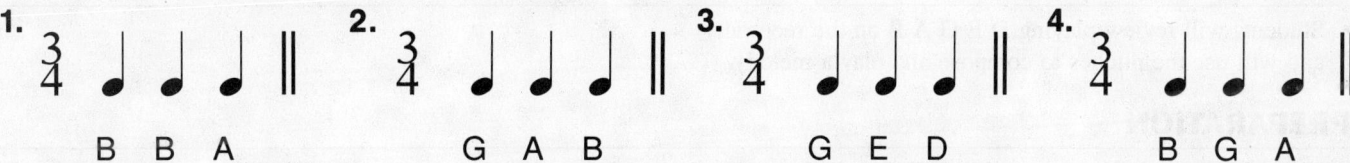

1. $\frac{3}{4}$ B B A
2. $\frac{3}{4}$ G A B
3. $\frac{3}{4}$ G E D
4. $\frac{3}{4}$ B G A

- Choose your favorite pattern from the four above, and write the letter names of those pitches in each circled measure below.

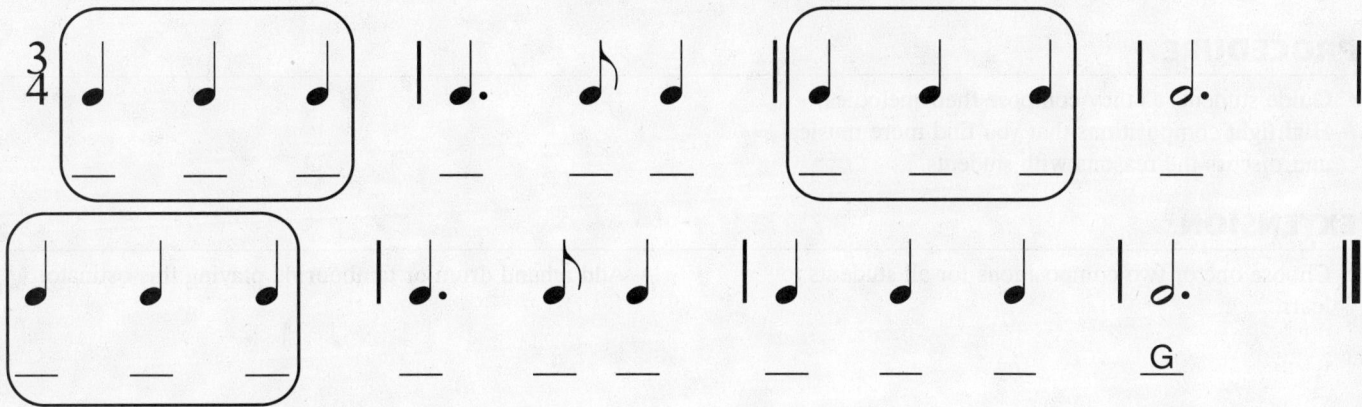

- Fill in the other blanks above with the letter names of pitches D E G A B to complete the melody. Then practice playing your melody.

- Play your melody for a friend. Then listen to the melody your friend composed. Talk about how your pieces are alike and how they are different.

- Write the melody you composed on the staffs below.

Challenge: Play "Swapping Song," on page 82 of your textbook. You will use pitches D E G A B.

Pitches: *D E G A B*

USING RECORDER MASTER R•26

OBJECTIVE

- Students will review playing D E G A B on the recorder and will use the pitches to compose and play a melody.

PREPARATION

- Have students echo patterns using D E G A B, for example:

1. $\frac{3}{4}$ 𝅘𝅥𝅭 𝅘𝅥𝅮 𝅘𝅥 | 𝅗𝅥. ‖
    G   G E D

2. $\frac{3}{4}$ 𝅘𝅥 𝅘𝅥 𝅘𝅥 | 𝅗𝅥. ‖
    B B A G

PROCEDURE

- Guide students as they compose their melodies. Highlight compositions that you find more musical, and discuss the reasons with students.

EXTENSION

- Choose one or two compositions for all students to learn.

- Add a hand drum or tambourine playing this ostinato:

$\frac{3}{4}$ 𝅘𝅥 𝅘𝅥 :‖

McGraw-Hill

Name_____

Planets in Outer Space with **D E G A**

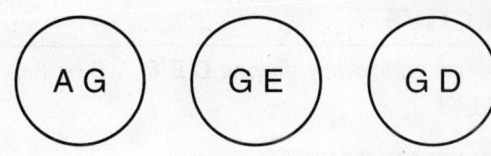

- Imagine that the circles on the right are pitch planets way out in space. Practice playing each of the two-pitch patterns shown on these planets, over and over as fast as you can.

- Now try the three-pitch patterns on these planets:

- Play a "Pitch Planet Guessing Game" with a friend: Your friend chooses and plays one of the two-pitch or three-pitch patterns on the planets, and you guess which pattern it is. Then switch roles. Continue until each of you has played all the planet patterns.

- Write the pitch letter name under each note on the staff below.

"This Pretty Planet" Accompaniment

- Now play the accompaniment above with "This Pretty Planet," on page 257 of your textbook.

Challenge: Play this mystery song. Then fill in the title.

Mystery Song:_____

Pitches: *D E G A B*

USING RECORDER MASTER R•27

OBJECTIVE

- Students will review playing D E G A B on the recorder.

PREPARATION

- Have students sing "This Pretty Planet," on page 257 of the textbook.

PROCEDURE

- Guide students in playing the "Pitch Planet Guessing Game."
- Have them complete the written activity:

  | A | G D G | E E G | G A |

- Have students practice the accompaniment. Then have a third of the class play the accompaniment while the rest of the class sings the song in unison.
- Have students play the mystery song and guess the title ("One More River").

EXTENSION

- Have students, in small groups, create a "music from outer space" introduction to "This Pretty Planet" using any recorder sounds they wish. Encourage them to try also vocal sounds and percussion-instrument sounds.

McGraw-Hill

In the King's Court with D E G A B

- Pat the rhythm below.

- Now play the rhythm above on pitch G.

- Write the pitch letter name under each note on the staffs below.

"The Court of King Carraticus" Fanfare

- With a friend, play the two parts of the fanfare together before The song "The Court of King Carraticus," on page 263 of your textbook. Imagine that you are playing as the king enters the throne room!

Challenge: Make up your own melody to the rhythm of the poem "Old King Cole." Use pitches D E G A B.

> Old King Cole was a merry old soul,
> And a merry old soul was he.
> He called for his pipe and he called for his bowl
> And he called for his fiddlers three.

Pitches: *D G E A B*

McGraw-Hill

USING RECORDER MASTER R•28

OBJECTIVE

- Students will review playing D E G A B on the recorder.

PREPARATION

- Have students echo four-beat patterns using D E G A B, for example:

1.

2.

PROCEDURE

- Guide students through the activities.
- As they practice the rhythm pattern, encourage students to lightly tongue the sixteenth notes.

- Have students complete the written activity:

  Part 1
  | GGGGAG | GGAG |
  Part 2
  | EEEEEE | DDDE |

- Then help them to form pairs and play the two parts of the fanfare together.

EXTENSION

- Have students act out the song "The Court of King Carraticus," on page 263 of the textbook. Have them choose a group of "royal recorder players" to play the fanfare parts as an interlude between verses.

"C" How Much Fun This Is!

- Practice playing Part 1 below.

Part 1

- Now play Part 1 with the refrain of "Simple Gifts," on page 269 of your textbook.

- Finger A on your recorder. Then lift the first finger of the left hand to finger C'.

C'

C'

- Practice playing each of the patterns shown in the boxes. Then play the patterns in order.

| A C' C' | A C' C' | A C' C' | C' C' C' |

- Write the patterns above on the following staff with the rhythm given.

Part 2

A C'   C'   A C'   C'   A C'   C'   C' C'   C'

- Play Part 2 above with the refrain of "Simple Gifts."

Challenge: Practice playing back and forth between B and C' and between G and C'. Then practice playing the melody of "Aquaqua," on page 219 of your textbook.

Pitches: E G A B C'

McGraw-Hill

USING RECORDER MASTER R•29

OBJECTIVE

- Students will learn to play C' on the recorder and will review E G A B.

PREPARATION

- Have students finger A on an "arm" recorder. Then have them lift the first finger, leaving the second finger in place. (See page 20 for more about the "arm" recorder.)

- Have students echo-sing the following patterns: A A A, A A C', A C' A.

PROCEDURE

- Guide students through the activities.
- In fingering C', encourage students to lift the first finger just slightly off the hole.

- Have students complete the written activity:

EXTENSION

- Have small groups of students play Parts 1 and 2 simultaneously while the rest of the class sings the refrain of "Simple Gifts," on page 269 of the textbook.

Name _____

Let's Meet Another D

- Finger C¹ on your recorder. Then lift the left thumb away from the thumb hole to finger D¹.

- Play the pattern on the right.

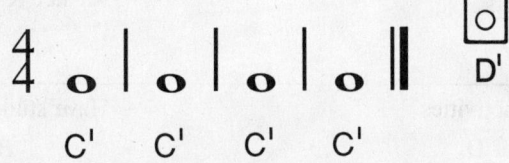

C¹ C¹ C¹ C¹

- Now change the pattern, and play this one:

C¹ D¹ C¹ C¹

- Write the pitch letter name under each note on the staffs below.

"This Pretty Planet" Accompaniment 2

Part 1

Play three times

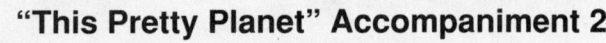

Part 2

- Now, with a friend, play both parts above as an accompaniment to "This Pretty Planet," on page 257 of your textbook.

Challenge: Work with a friend to compose your own "Planet" song, 8 or 16 measures long. Use any of the rhythms ♫ ♩ 𝄽 ♩ 𝅗𝅥 and any of the pitches you have learned: D E G A B C¹ D¹. Notate the song on staff paper, and write a title and your names above it. Practice playing the song with your friend. Then play it for the rest of the class.

Pitches: D E G A B C¹ D¹

McGraw-Hill

USING RECORDER MASTER R•30

OBJECTIVE

- Students will learn to play D' on the recorder and will review D E G A B C'.

PREPARATION

- Have students sing the song "This Pretty Planet," on page 257 of the textbook.

- Have some students play the accompaniment on Recorder Master R•27 while the others sing the song.

PROCEDURE

- Guide students through the activities.
- Demonstrate the fingering for D'.
- Encourage students to keep the right hand close to, but not touching, the recorder when playing C' and D'.

- Have students complete the written activity:

  Part 1
  | C' | D' | C' | C' |
  Part 2
  | A | G D G | E E G | G A |

EXTENSION

- Have students play the "Pitch Planet Guessing Game" from Recorder Master R•27 using two- and three-pitch patterns on D E G A B C' D'. Have them suggest the patterns. Write these on the chalkboard.

McGraw-Hill

Name_____

Melodies to Play for a Friend (Page 1)

● Play these melodies using the pitches you know.

Taps

Traditional

Old MacDonald Had a Farm

Traditional

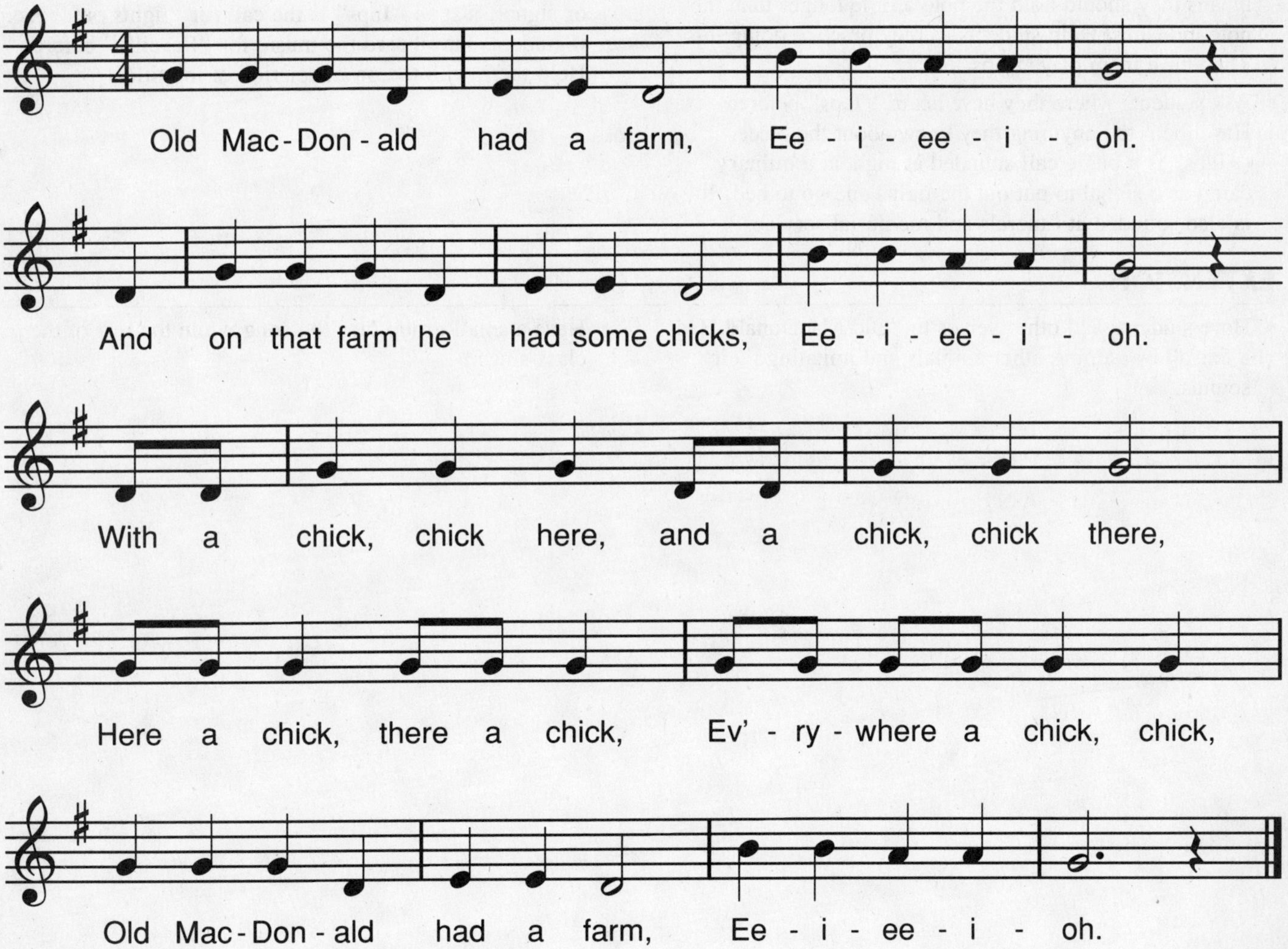

Old Mac - Don - ald   had   a   farm,   Ee - i - ee - i - oh.

And   on that farm he   had some chicks,   Ee - i - ee - i - oh.

With   a   chick,   chick   here,   and   a   chick,   chick   there,

Here   a   chick,   there   a   chick,   Ev' - ry - where   a   chick,   chick,

Old   Mac - Don - ald   had   a   farm,   Ee - i - ee - i - oh.

Pitches: D E G A B D'

McGraw-Hill

USING RECORDER MASTER R•31 (Pages 1 and 2)

OBJECTIVE

• Students will review playing D E G A B D' on the recorder and will use the pitches to play melodies.

PREPARATION

• Have students review the fingerings for D E G A B D'.

PROCEDURE

• Guide students as they clap the rhythm of each melody and then sing or say the letter names of the pitches in rhythm while fingering the pitches on the recorder. Then have them play each melody.

• Point out to students the symbol over the last note in "Taps," and tell them that this is a *fermata,* which means they should hold the note a little longer than the note indicates. Help students as they practice doing this. Then have them play "Taps."

• Ask students where they have heard "Taps" before. Have them tell anything they know about the piece. ("Taps" is a bugle call sounded at night at a military camp as a signal to put out the lights and go to bed. It is also sounded at funerals and memorial services.)

• Have students practice and play "Old MacDonald Had a Farm."

• Have them practice the pattern at the top of page 2 of the recorder master. Then have students practice and play "Reveille."

• Discuss with students that "Reveille" is a wake-up call or signal, just as "Taps" is the call for "lights out." Ask if students have heard the music for "Reveille" before. Help them with the pronunciation of the title.

EXTENSION

• Have students add other verses to "Old MacDonald Had a Farm" by naming other animals and imitating their sounds.

• Have a small group play the song while the rest of the class sings it.

Melodies to Play for a Friend (Page 2)

- Practice playing the following pattern.

- Now play the following melody, which uses the pattern above.

Reveille

U.S. Army Bugle Call

End
(Fine)

Go back to the beginning
and play to the end
(Da Capo al Fine)

Pitches: D E G A B D¹

All Around the House with G A C¹ D¹

- Play each of the four parts on the staffs below.

- Compare Parts 1 and 2 above with Parts 3 and 4. How are they alike? How are they different?

- Choose a friend to play the parts with. Decide whether you will play Parts 1 and 2 or Parts 3 and 4. One of you play Part 1 or 3, the other play Part 2 or 4. Play the parts together.

- Now play your parts together with the verse of "Old Joe Clark," on page 260 of your textbook.

Challenge: Play the refrain of "Old Joe Clark" below. You will begin on pitch G.

"Old Joe Clark" Refrain

Pitches: D G A B C¹ D¹

USING RECORDER MASTER R•32

OBJECTIVE

- Students will review playing D G A B C' D' on the recorder.

PREPARATION

- Have students echo four-beat patterns on C' and D', for example:

$$\frac{4}{4}\ \downarrow \quad \downarrow \quad \overline{}\ \downarrow \quad \|$$

C'   D'   C' D' C'

- Draw Old Joe Clark's house on the chalkboard—a house with 16 floors, each floor labeled with a pattern, reading from top to bottom: **1.** C' C'; **2.** C' C' C'; **3.** C' C'; **4.** C' C' C'; **5.** A A; **6.** A A G; **7.** A A; **8.** A G A; **9.** C' C' D' C'; **10.** C' C' D' C'; **11.** C' C' D' C'; **12.** C' D' C' D' C'; **13.** A A A G A; **14.** A A G A G; **15.** A A A G A; **16.** A G A.

- Have students practice playing each pattern in Old Joe Clark's house, starting from the top floor.

PROCEDURE

- Guide students through the activities.
- Discuss with them the similarities and differences between the parts. (Parts 3 and 4 are ornamented versions of Parts 1 and 2.)
- Point out to students that they will begin the refrain of "Old Joe Clark" on a different pitch from the one shown on textbook page 260.

EXTENSION

- Have students choose any four patterns from Old Joe Clark's house to combine into an original melody. Have them write down their melodies and play them for each other.

McGraw-Hill

Theme and Variations

- Play the theme of "Hot Cross Buns" below.

Hot Cross Buns

Traditional

- Now try this variation. How is it similar to the theme and how is it different from it?

- Play Variation 2 below with two friends. Each of you play one part.

Challenge: Now play the variation below, which uses quarter notes, eighth notes, and sixteenth notes.

Pitches: D G A B C' D'

USING RECORDER MASTER R•33

OBJECTIVE

- Students will review playing D G A B C' D' on the recorder.

PREPARATION

- Have students stand facing a partner, with their hands on each other's shoulders, and seesaw up and down. Demonstrate with the "arm" recorder that the first two fingers of the left hand seesaw between B and C'. (See page 10 for more about the "arm" recorder.)

PROCEDURE

- Guide students as they practice and perform the theme and variations. Have them identify the basic melody of "Hot Cross Buns" in each variation.
- Discuss with students the similarity and differences between the theme and Variation 1. (Variation 1 has the same melody as the theme, but different meter and rhythm.)
- Assign four groups of recorder players, one to the theme and one to each of the variations. Have the groups play in the order on the page, ending with the first group repeating the theme. (Note that Variation 2 has three parts to be played together.)

EXTENSION

- Have students compose variations on the melody of "Fais do-do" from Recorder Master R•22.

McGraw-Hill

Name_____

Songs for a Recorder Concert (Page 1)

- Play these songs using the pitches you know.

Hush, Little Baby

Southern U.S. Folk Song

Hush, lit-tle ba-by, Don't say a word, Pa-pa's going to buy you a mock-ing-bird.

If that mock-ing - bird won't sing, Pa-pa's going to buy you a dia-mond ring.

Lightly Row

Folk Song

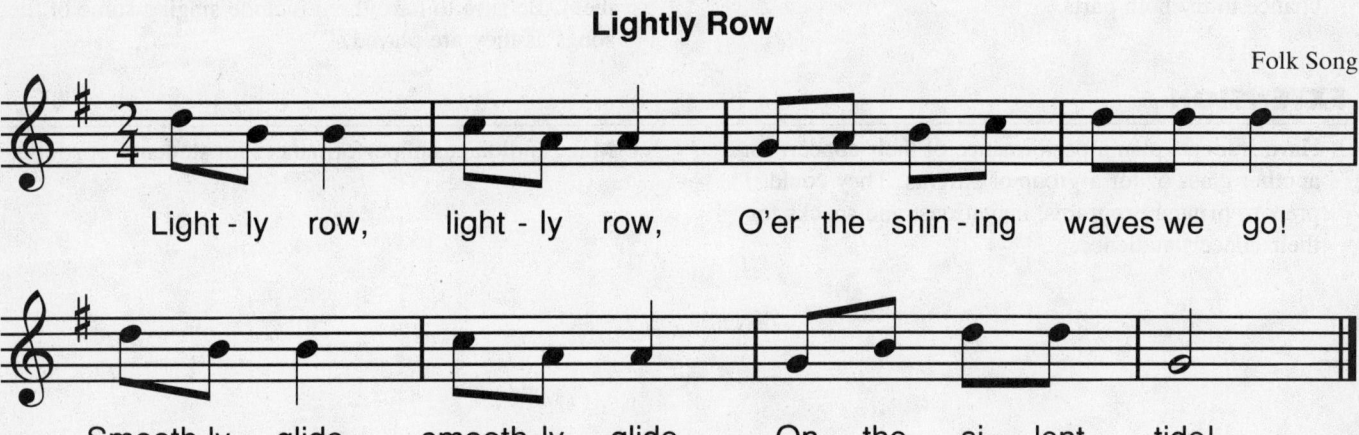

Light - ly row, light - ly row, O'er the shin - ing waves we go!

Smooth-ly glide, smooth-ly glide, On the si - lent tide!

- When you have learned this harmony part, you will be ready to play a duet with a friend. One of you play "Lightly Row" while the other plays the harmony part. Then switch parts and play again.

"Lightly Row" Harmony Part

Pitches: D G A B C¹ D¹

OBJECTIVE

- Students will play songs on the recorder using D G A B C' D' and will plan a recorder concert using songs they have learned throughout the year.

PREPARATION

- Have students review the fingering for D G A B C' D'.

PROCEDURE

- Have students practice and play the pieces on page 1 of the recorder master.

- You may wish to have the class play the duet before students try it with a partner. Divide the class into two groups and have each group play one of the parts of the duet. Have groups switch parts so that all students get a chance to try both parts.

- Have students practice and play the songs "Go Tell Aunt Rhody" and "Jingle Bells" on page 2 of the recorder master.

- Then have students plan a recorder concert with selected songs that they have learned throughout the year. Have them suggest the songs and then make a plan for presenting them. Be sure to have them include singing some of the songs as they are played.

EXTENSION

- Have students plan a performance of their concert for another class or for a group of parents. They could prepare printed programs, invitations, and snacks for their concert audience.

- Make audiotapes of performances for students' portfolios.

Songs for a Recorder Concert (Page 2)

- Play these songs using the pitches you know.

Go Tell Aunt Rhody

Folk Song

Go   tell   Aunt   Rho - dy,   Go   tell   Aunt   Rho - dy,

Go   tell   Aunt   Rho - dy the   old   gray goose is   dead.

Jingle Bells

J. Pierpont

Jin - gle   bells,   jin - gle   bells,   jin - gle   all   the   way!

Oh, what fun   it   is   to   ride   in   a   one-horse o - pen   sleigh! __

Jin - gle   bells,   jin - gle   bells,   jin - gle   all   the   way!

Oh, what fun   it   is   to   ride   in   a   one-horse o - pen   sleigh.

- When you have practiced these songs, play them for friends.

Pitches: D G A B C^I D^I

CELEBRATIONS

The material in this Celebrations section is to accompany the Celebrations lessons in the textbook or the Teacher's Edition of SHARE THE MUSIC. As your students acknowledge the various holidays by singing the following songs, you may wish to have them perform these recorder activities.

Pitches needed to play the Celebrations recorder pieces have been indicated for each selection. If pitches have not been introduced at the time you wish to use a recorder piece, you may wish to teach them at this time. Charts have been provided on the inside back cover of this book for all fingerings needed.

There are no teaching suggestions pages for these recorder masters, but the following general teaching instructions apply to all lessons.

1. Demonstrate the fingering for any new pitches that students will need, and help students to master the pitches.
2. Guide students in their practice of the melodies and countermelodies.
3. Assist in the forming of groups for the various activities.

CELEBRATIONS

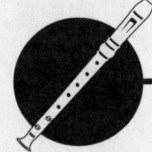

America

- Learn the descant below for "America," on page 302 of your textbook, using pitches A C' D'.

"America" Descant

Carol King

- Form a group of recorder players, and play the descant while others sing the song.

Pitches: A C' D'

Name

The Ghost of John

- Learn to play each part of the two-part pattern for "The Ghost of John" using pitches E G A B. Form two recorder groups, and play the parts together as an introduction and coda for the song, on page 306 of your textbook.

"The Ghost of John" Pattern

Introduction and Coda

Carol King

- Improvise an interlude on E G A B. Make it as long as the song. Play your interlude between repetitions of the song, either as a solo or with a group.

Pitches: E G A B

RECORDER MASTER R•37

Dry Bones

- The song "Dry Bones" is on page 308 of your textbook. Use pitches G A B to play the melody of the last three lines of the song as others sing the words.

- Now learn to play the following countermelody for the last three lines of the song using pitches G A B.

"Dry Bones" Countermelody

- Form two groups of recorder players, and play the last three lines of the song and the countermelody together.

Pitches: G A B

A Mince Pie or Pudding

- Learn to play the following descant for "A Mince Pie or Pudding" using pitches D and E. Then play the descant as other students sing the song, on page 311 of your textbook. Switch roles and repeat the song.

"A Mince Pie or Pudding" Descant

Marilyn Davidson

Pitches: D E

In the Window

- Play this countermelody for "In the Window" using pitches D G A.

"In the Window" Countermelody

Carol King

- Form a group, and play the countermelody as others sing the song, on page 316 of your textbook. Then switch parts and repeat.

Pitches: D G A

Dale, dale, dale!

- Learn to play both parts of the two-part accompaniment for
  the refrain of "Dale, dale, dale!" using pitches D E G A.
  Choose a friend, and play both parts of the accompaniment
  as a duet.

"Dale, dale, dale!" Accompaniment

- Now play the accompaniment as others sing the refrain, on
  page 322 of your textbook.

- Play the refrain of "Dale, dale, dale!" using pitches E G A B C¹.

Pitches: *D E G A B C¹*

McGraw-Hill

Name_____

We Three Kings

- Create an introduction to "We Three Kings," on page 329 of your textbook. Use pitches E G A B and the following rhythm.

- Write your introduction on the staff below.

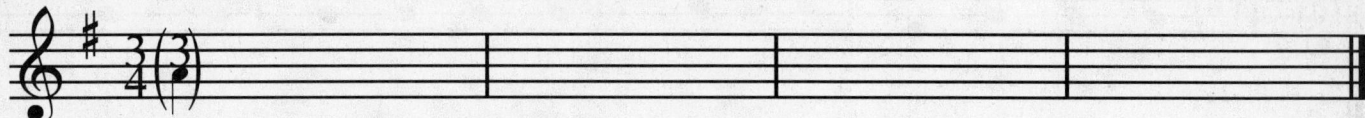

- Form a group of recorder players, and play your introduction before others sing the song. Listen to the introductions composed by others in your group. Have the group choose one they like and play it for the class.

- Play the refrain of "We Three Kings," starting with the second measure, using pitches D E G A B C'.

Pitches: *D E G A B* C'

McGraw-Hill

Name _____

Down by the Riverside

- The song "Down by the Riverside" is on page 338 of your textbook. Learn the following descant for the refrain using pitches D E G.

"Down by the Riverside" Descant

Carol King

- Form a group of recorder players, and play the descant with the refrain as others sing. Switch players and repeat.

- Play the refrain of the song using pitches G A B C$^\text{I}$. Then form two groups of recorder players, and play the refrain and the descant together.

Pitches: D E G A B C$^\text{I}$